Imagems 1

THE SHEARSMAN CHAPBOOK SERIES, 2013

Martin Anderson *The Lower Reaches*
Richard Berengarten *Imagems 1*
Susan Connolly *The Sun-Artist*
Amy Evans *The Sea Quells*
Alice Kavounas *Thin Ice*
Tin Ujević *Twelve Poems (translated by Richard Berengarten)*

Imagems 1

Richard Berengarten

Shearsman Books

First published in the United Kingdom in 2013 by
Shearsman Books, 50 Westons Hill Drive, Emersons Green
BRISTOL BS16 7DF

Shearsman Books Ltd Registered Office
30–31 St. James Place, Mangotsfield, Bristol BS16 9JB
(this address not for correspondence)

www.shearsman.com

ISBN 978-1-84861-312-6

Acknowledgements

Thanks to the editors of the following journals, in which these texts have appeared: 'The Dialectics of Oxygen', *Jacket* 40, http://jacketmagazine.com/40/berengarten-dialectics.shtml, and *World Poetry almanac 2009*, Ulaanbaatar, Mongolia, 2010; 'A Little Further?', http://www.berengarten.com/site/A-little-further.html, and bilingual Spanish-English version, trs. Miguel Teruel Pozas and Paul S. Derrick, *Serta* 9, UNED (Universidad Nacional de Educación a Distancia); 'On poetry and magnanimity', *Martlet*, issue 13, spring 2009, Pembroke College, Cambridge; and 'On Poetry and Glory (1)', 'On Poetry and Glory (2)' and 'On Poetry and Catching Glories', *The Long Poem Magazine*, N° 7, 2012. Many thanks also to Melanie Rein and Anthony Rudolf for their constant support. The cover shows a sketch of the author made by Marin Sorescu in Belgrade, 1982.

Contents

For the first time in our history we are contemporaries of all humanity.

OCTAVIO PAZ

A little further
we shall see the almond trees in blossom
the marble glistening in the sun
the waves breaking

a little further,
let us rise up a little higher

GEORGE SEFERIS

A Little Further?

Twelve propositions

1. There are no temporal or spatial centres. Everywhere/everywhen is both centre and periphery. Octavio Paz answered Yeats' complaint that "the centre cannot hold" (1919), with the assertion that "for the first time in our history, we are contemporaries of all humanity" (1950).

2. After Paz, it's no longer enough to break down borders merely within and for any sub-group. All ethnicities belong any/everywhere. Poetry is universal. There is no civilization without poetry. Every tradition is an open, appreciable secret, belonging to whoever discovers and learns it.

3. Reading Paz this way moves (re-turns) us to the vatic and shamanic origins of poetry and to the Orphic responsibilities that Blake and Shelley were the last English poets to advocate with wholehearted spirit and sustained devotion. "All humanity" means not only the living, but the dead and the unborn.

4. A poet has responsibilities: social as well as subjective, communal as well as individual. Any emphasis on 'spirituality' in poetry, if it is not to caricature or betray itself, needs to involve critical commitment within, to and for both the past and future history of "all humanity", and all nature.

5. Languages have gaps and holes and render reality imperfectly. To make a poem, a poet needs to travel through them into silence and to return through them from silence back into language: to test (tear) the boundaries between language and silence. This two-way movement between language

and silence means that every poetic journey is a Heracleitan return, not a one-way flight.

6. A term like 'beyond' confirms and embodies the spatio-temporal basis of reality, with all its binary distinctions, and is inconceivable without/outwith it. Can a shaman or seer, let alone a word-spinning poet, surpass such spatiotemporal constraints by moving, or at least peering, 'further into' any such 'beyond'? The Lurianic Cabbalists studied this and answered: *Not through the last Veil, and no more than in sparks and glimpses.* Apparently the masters of the *Dao de jing* liberated themselves from binary distinctions only by neatly stepping in and through the gaps and holes of paradox. *Question*: What is the sound of one hand clapping? *Answer*: Poetry.

7. Poetry is a challenge to mortality and a criticism of Death. Crossing deaths, poems are spacetime-travellers: they encapsulate a non-self-defeating irony, the only defeat Death might admit, if Death had words.

8. Ancient laws of reciprocity, hospitality and magnanimity are necessary to the poetry of *this* time and *this* place too. Anything else or less is not good enough and will not serve adequately. A poet without such qualities can only be second-rate, however clever, skilled and cunning.

9. Poets who think of themselves literal-mindedly as belonging to *either* 'central' *or* conversely 'peripheral' positions are *both* likely to achieve little more than provincial nowherehood. Paz's call demands wholehearted pluralism, eclecticism and multiculturalism. Here, the word *wholehearted* is not accidental. Who wants or needs a heartless (or headless) poetry?

10. A poetry informed by Paz's perspectives is less likely to be parochial than one that isn't. While poetry can't support itself

without embodiment, awareness that the universal dwells in the particular and the particular in the universal *breeds* hospitality and magnanimity: poetry thrives on respect and affection for alterities.

11. Whenever the guest arrives, the host is reciprocally hosted. The particular interior that encompasses both guest and host is the anterior timespace that itself first gave welcome to the host. Poetry, being itself a gift, flourishes in that generous presence of arrivals, meetings and gift-givings.

12. We might learn our theory and practice from a Southern African word: Archbishop Desmond Tutu writes: the "word *Ubuntu* ... speaks about about the essence of being human: that my humanity is caught up in your humanity because we say a person is a person through other persons. I am a person because I belong. The same is true of you" (1998).

The Dialectics of Oxygen

Twelve propositions

1. These are the dialectics of oxygen.

2. Breath is the condition of air in and among the living.

3. To share breath is to share love and justice.

4. Breath is the ground of being and the core of poetry.

5. Find breath (air, wind) and (you will, you may) stand anywhere in spacetime.

6. A breath is a balance and an exchange poised on the fulcrum of being. This for that, tit for tat. Animals on one side, plants on the other. A perfectly tuned economy, a perfectly patterned ergonomy. Tick-tock. A metronome. In all winds and weathers. In all airs.

7. A single breath is a full (complete) wave. Breathing is the tide of life.

8. Since breath is what happens to air when it moves in and out of the living, in and out of life, the margins of breathing and not-breathing distinguish life from not-life.

9. Breath is coterminous with life. Breath means (characterises, defines) the condition life. Breath equals (is) life. Without breath, no life. Without breathing, no living.

10. The dead are (consist of), simply, all those who have ever breathed. Breath is our mortal (deathly) condition in spacetime. What we, the living, share with all the dead, as

with all the as-yet-unborn, who are (even, also) once to live, is the condition (of) breath a while.

11. Consider: (once-upon-a-spacetime) I who made this did so breathing. As do and may you do now, receiving it.

12. For the entire duration of spacetime, the condition (of) breathing is (equals) the common miracle.

On Poetry and Glory (1)

Twelve propositions

1. Glory is directly apprehensible as a quality that is inherent in things and belongs to them.

2. Glory is an open secret, always available, ever-ready. It is a *datum* of life: a gift given. It is in nature and is natural. You don't have to travel far, even at all, to find, reach, hear, see glory. It is here, now. And it is both unique and multiple, unrepeatable and continual, instantaneous and continuous, singular and plural, *datum* and *data*. Glory occurs here, in-here. It sticks to things; it sticks around. It adheres and it inheres.

3. Glory can be hard to separate from things. But since we humans are at once gifted and limited to living in a smellable, tasteable, tangible, audible and visible world, finitely set and beset in infinite spacetime, is there any reason why anyone would even wish to enforce any such separation?

4. Which is also to say: if glory does have an intrinsic core, this is likely to be indescribable and uncapturable. The core of glory is approachable only in and through its manifestation(s): inklings, hints, suggestions, glimmerings, veils, appearances.

5. Even so, glory isn't entirely inseparable from the world 'out there' and can sometimes be perceived/experienced as a phenomenon in its own right – or, rather, *almost* in its own right, apparently momentarily loosened from things and independent of them.

6. When the visual sense is in question and predominant, as it so often is, this 'loosening' of glory occurs especially in the skies, and especially at dawns, sunsets and dusks, and/or wherever objects, liquid or solid, and sky (light and qualities of light) interact. For example on horizons, and following the contours of trees, hills and mountains, and in and among shifting reflections and refractions, especially on water, and anywhere where there are prismatic effects, and in flickerings through gradations of shadow. And in the sheens on things, and their textures. And especially in movement, for example, when a wind is blowing, and when one is travelling fast, and things 'rush by'.

7. So, perhaps it would be more accurate to say: glory happens (occurs, is manifest, is experienced) at edges, border zones, thresholds, frontiers, that mark both spatial and temporal transitions, whether stark and rapid or gradual and nuanced, between physical (tangible, palpable, apparent, immanent etc.) realities and inklings/apperceptions of realities that are metaphysical (impalpable, intangible, transcendental, etc.). Which is to say: glory is liminal.

8. The apprehension or experience of glory is also ephemeral. Its occurrence or arrival, often surprising and unexpected, may even be regarded as the defining property of the instant, the *Augenblick* (German 'moment'; literally 'eyeblink'). Glory is itself and what-it-is-in-itself, and nothing else than what-it-is, even though the presence or intimation of elseness or otherness irrevocably forms half of its core.

9. When glory arrives it usually disappears at the precise moment you apprehend it. It is not 'just' that it is fleeting. It is that glory is itself the heart or core of transformation. Glory is that which changes in change: it is the 'changingness' of change. Glory is *quick*, in both the word's meanings: 'alive' and 'fast'. And, also in both meanings of *fast*: not only 'swift-moving' but also, paradoxically, 'firmly adhering'.

10. Each particular occurrence or manifestation of glory is unique and unrepeatable, even though it is likely to have an echo. Even though it may be many-chambered and voluminous, and so have many echoes. Even though it may be possessed and dispossessed by multiple memories and premonitions, by manifold after-ripples and forecastings. And even though it may transform into other manifestations: colossal continuums, strings harmonised in polyphonies, linked chains of glories.

11. There is, in fact and in deed, both an immediate *thisness* (*hereness*, *nowness*) and an uncanny *elseness* (*thereness*, *otherness*) to glory. Its quality is – or rather, its qualities are – experiencable as ordinary and extraordinary at once: real *and* fantastic, mundane *and* magical/marvellous; merely commonplace/quotidian on the one hand *and* queerly eerie/weirdly wonderful on the other. Glory simultaneously binds and opens matter and mind to the spiritual, the sacral, the numinous:

    Voices in the mirror call
    the commonplace *is* miracle.

12. When glory resonates and/or shines in (on, into, through, over, around, out of, etc) language, the result is poetry.

On Poetry and Glory (2)

Twelve Propositions

1. In the apperception or intimation of glory, this human frame, the container of this being in the here-and-now, becomes a recipient (vessel, cup, bowl, etc.) for a fluid otherness, a volatile elseness.

2. The experience of glory has two complementary and oppositional components. One is the experience of movement – of being moved, in, through and within the flow of the here-and-now. The other is that of utter stillness and quietness.

3. The sensations of being filled – with awe, fear, wonder, beauty and so on – are the radicals of glory, as is evident from such inadequate verbal attempts at encapsulation as aw*ful*, fear*ful*, wonder*ful*, beauti*ful*. And what is more, the sense of filling may exceed the *ful*filling. Glory may flood and engulf.

4. The movements that glory precipitates are not only of flowing (pouring, streaming, flooding, etc.), but also of pulsation, wave-motion, exchange (up and down, in and out). So glory occurs not only in filling and being filled but, equally, in emptying and being emptied – as in breathing (inspiration/release); and as in the innumerable fluted, fluent, nuanced patternings and transformations of erotic love.

5. The movement of glory can be both centrifugal and centripetal. Glory both contracts/intensifies to a point and expands/ spreads concentrically. Glory heightens and deepens. Glory is uplifting but may equally be giddying and dizzying. Glory can also be weighted, heavily downpulling.

6. The complementary component of glory, that of stillness and quietness, involves total acquiescence in being outside/ outwith place-and-time (locatedness) *at the same time as* being inside it, in its verity, its very-ness.

7. So glory involves (dialectical) conjunction of presence and absence, of action and passion, of gift / giving and reception / receiving, of emptiness and fullness, of movement upwards and downwards, and of movement and stillness. And, also, of guesting and hosting.

8. Glory and beauty are aspects of each other – as in ☯, the diagram of the *Taiji tu* ['Great Ultimate']. Although both can simultaneously move and be still, neither can be grasped, let alone tamed, possessed, measured or hoarded. Try to employ/deploy either glory or beauty, and each will turn instantaneously into something else, corrupt, fizzle out, rot, shrivel, die. Or perhaps even transform into its diabolic opposite and turn snarling against its abuser, superhumanly maniacal in destructive power. So end empires. Use (utilisation, usage) of glory and beauty automatically means their wearing down, their *misuse* – and worse, their *abuse*.

9. Glory and beauty are both, literally, *breath*taking. Both may breed terror. Both demand awe. Both are defiant, uncommandable and, in totality and essence, free. Rainer Maria Rilke, who knew all this, expressed it better than anyone:

> For Beauty's nothing
> but beginning of Terror we're still just able to bear,
> and why we adore it so is because it serenely
> disdains to destroy us.

10. In saying anything about glory, everything to do with it wants to be said at once, to be blurted out, cascading, as in a waterfall, an onrush, a spontaneous flood, a downpour,

and simultaneously to ripple and circle back upon itself, rounding and surrounding itself, re-amalgamating and re-adhering with itself and reabsorbing itself, into a kind of polyvocal chant, a symphonic choral simultaneity.

11. These observations about some factors underlying verbal expression reflect the nonverbal and preverbal experience of glory. But the *Gestalten* (patternings) parcelled in oral language are held together by threads and strings of linear time. So the necessarily sequential delivery of language itself doesn't do justice to that pressured insistence, cannot encapsulate or encompass such instantaneously composite and all-inclusive flooding. What is being said in this present piece of writing is constrained by precisely these overwhelmings. (Constrained and also contained?) Writing, being even more bound to linearity than speech, strains to its utmost limits to accommodate glory.

12. Except in poetry. Which achieves the near-impossible by its synchronous polygonal bombardment of linear sequences of thought-in-language/language-in-thought – with its unheralded curves, twists and zigzags, its stark sudden soarings and sheer precipitous tumblings, its unexpected complexities and unimagined affinities, its radiant heuristic leaps and unforeseen openings, and its as-yet-untold heraldings and astonishing, delightful and unenvisaged panoramic clarities.

On Poetry and Catching Glories

Twelve propositions

1. Glories are the sounds and sheens of phenomena, glimpsed or overheard in and from their surfaces.

2. Such glimpsing or overhearing is always direct, always personal, as if their surfaces were faces.

3. As if *in* and as if *from* their open eyes and mouths. As if all things had mouths and eyes. And could be listened to and communicated with, directly, in mutual and acceptant quietness, in quiescence. Even actually in silence.

4. As if the entire world we live, and live in, were animated: that is to say, *ensouled.*

5. Is the tentative 'as if' actually necessary in the preceding clauses? Not, I think, for a poet. Not, I think, for poetry. At the very least, poetry holds each 'as-if-ness' in temporary abeyance; that is to say, in a "willing suspension of disbelief". Or in a *suspense* of disbelief?

6. The Greek verb *φαίνειν* [*phaínein*] means "show, pass, be seen, appear" (Onions, 674); "to make bright, to shine", "from the base *φαν*-, lengthened form of *φα*-, to shine" (Skeat, 439). The passive form, *φαίνομαι* [*phaínomai*] means "to be shewn, to appear" (ibid). The adjective *φανερός* [*fanerós*] means "visible, clear" (Onions, 674), hence 'apparent'. The corresponding noun, *φαινόμενον* [*phainómenon*], i.e. 'appearance', 'that which is evident, that which happens', is formed from the neuter form of the passive participle of *φαίνειν*. Hence our word 'phenomenon', whose prime meaning the *Compact Edition* of the *Oxford*

English Dictionary (*OED*) offers elegantly as: "a thing that appears, or is perceived or observed; an individual fact, occurrence, or change as perceived by any of the senses, or by the mind [...]" (*OED*, 772). Hence also our words *epiphany*, "manifestation of a supernatural being" (Onions, 320) and *theophany*, "manifestation of God or a god to man" (*OED*, 277) – both also from *φαίνειν*. So, a phenomenon is an 'appearance', and an 'epiphany'. Both reveal glories.

7. Glimpsed or overheard, grazed or glanced at, brushed or touched, scented or tasted – however broached – once even merely intimated, glory converts instantaneously into appetite, desire and hope – and, from these, into 'impulse or impetus for good' and thence into 'action for good': that is, תיקון [*tikkun*].

8. This Hebrew word has many meanings, including "a perfecting, a betterment, and a correction, though in other contexts it may mean an institution or arrangement" (Scholem 1969, 127). In this sense, תיקון *tikkun* may be said to mean 'repair, mend, fix' and possibly 'heal'. In the Kabbalah, more specifically, it means: "harmonious correction and mending of the flaw" (ibid, 110); "restoration" (ibid, 113), and "not so much a restoration of Creation [...] as its first complete fulfilment" (ibid, 117). I would add to Scholem's qualification: "as its first complete glory".

9. *Tikkun* as the restitution and/or fulfilment of the glory of creation is the hope, aspiration, goal, target of the *work* that is poetry and that poetry involves and demands.

10. Poetry *catches* the sheen and sound of glory in the here-and-now – in, between and among words, and between words and phenomena. That is to say, in the words themselves and also at all their borders and interfaces – with each other (when two); with one another (when more than two); and with the non-linguistic universe that is both 'out there' and

‘in here’, which is itself by definition not only the source of glory but also ineffable and speechless.

11. “Poetry *catches*...” This *catching* includes all senses and contexts of the English verb: (i) unwittingly, as one catches something contagious (e.g. laughing, yawning, a mood or, unfortunately, a virus); (ii) whether by chance or conscious effort, as one catches something that is not necessarily obvious (e.g. a hint, a clue, an undertone, an implication, a suggestion, a purport, an intention, a meaning); (iii) deliberately, as one catches something thrown or dropped, before it lands elsewhere (e.g. a ball, a leaf); (iv) equally deliberately, as one catches a creature that one has been searching for or hunting (a lion, a fish, a butterfly); (v) or as one can be caught unawares (in a situation, by a memory), etc.

12. So *catching glory* or *catching glories* is not a bad definition of what poetry does. And is.

On Poetry and Magnanimity

Twelve Propositions

1. The best poems have a quality of inherent magnanimity as well as of crystal clarity, verbal precision, conceptual economy, and the precisely nuanced registration and mapping of feeling.

2. To do its proper work, a poem needs finesse in technique. But without magnanimity, such finesse remains shell-like, a frame or container, polished but uninventive, veneered but arbitrary, possibly fashionable but lifeless or listless, and lacking relevance, meaning or depth.

3. Poetry is a form of action in language. Magnanimity in action, both in and out of language, is immediately recognisable in the simplest and most direct human terms. It communicates and it resonates. It does so universally. It is not just that it 'involves' the common touch. It is and consists of "the common miracle" that happens inevitably in and through the common touch.

4. Etymologies are telling. Magnanimity means not just generosity and compassion but *great-souledness*. Our Latinate word is paralleled in modern Greek (μεγαλοψυχία – megalo-psychía) and in modern Slavonic languages (e.g. Serbian, velikodušnost / великодушност). German has Grossherzigkeit – *great-heartedness*, just as in Hebrew, רוחב לב/rochav lev – *wide-heartedness*.

5. A great soul and a great heart: keys to action: keys to poetry. Poetry occurs whenever magnanimity happens in, to and through language. Conversely, magnanimity in, to and through language breeds poetry.

6. Magnanimity is heuristic: it is and consists in a finding, a discovery, an un-covering, a dis-closing, an opening-up. When it comes, it appears spontaneously, as a wave, a surprise, a gift. An onrush.

7. Surprise happens first for the giver and, second, transmits itself to the recipient. While transmission can be slowed down to a rate of fluctuation so slight as to be humanly indiscernible – and even to seem or be frozen and, so, to miss out generations – there may equally be a zero time-gap between its giving and its receiving. Caught in the double cone of pastness and futurity, magnanimity may travel at the speed of light. At the speed of love.

8. An act of magnanimity involves (evolves) as-yet-unreckonable releases of energy.

9. Magnanimity is curative. Magnanimity flowing in poems involves healing, תיקון [*tikkun*]: of hearts, souls, spirits. Why else should the services of poems be so universally called on to disclose births, baptisms and weddings and to enclose deaths in funerals? These functions of rounding off, surrounding, confirming and sealing once belonged to priest-poets. Through the magnanimities of their art, the finest poets today, heirs of shamanic psychopomps, are still the most effective ministrants.

10. Magnanimity 'happens' (occurs, arrives, 'arises') in writing when the will lets go and follows what is *all ready* and what is *already*: that is to say, already *out there*, already *in here*, and *ready* in the sense of 'alert, alerted' and 'of-itself-willing'. Although the practice of magnanimity can be prepared for, by long training and practice, it cannot be arbitrarily willed. Nor can it be faked. Meanness is self-evident. It mars poets, flaws poems.

11. Auden wrote: “Poetry makes nothing happen.” The conventional construal of this aphorism is that ‘poetry has no effect on or in the world.’ But a diametrically opposite interpretation is possible: that poetry turns a nothing into a happening, a no-thing (nonentity) into a contextualised event and meaning: which is also to say, into eventfulness and meanings. Poetry involves a demiurgic act: it makes the word (makes manifest the word) out of (nearly) nothing, out of (almost) anything.

12. A poem is polysemous: it presents (manifests) multiple meanings latent in a single, singular truth. These meanings are *here*, are *there*, for the giving and the taking. A poem’s plural meanings radiate from its central core. They spread radially, at once possessed and dispossessed by the magnanimity of a light source.

Notes

Title

I have coined the term 'imagem' with the meaning 'nexus, web, net, body, corpus, etc., of integrally associated ideas and images'. An *imagem* is composite, complex and polyesemic. It also implies 'unit of imagery', comparable to the word *mythologem* ('unit of myth or mythology', or, as defined by the *Oxford English Dictionary* online, "fundamental theme or motif of myth or other discourse"). I think such a term is helpful in English because it fills a conceptual gap. Shortly after arriving at this term, together with its first, tentative definition, I discovered that it already exists in Portuguese, meaning, simply, *image*.

Epigraphs

1. Octavio Paz, *The Labyrinth of Solitude*, tr. Lysander Kemp, Allen Lane, the Penguin Press, London, 1967, p. 182; original Spanish version first published in *Cuadernos Americanos*, 1950. Translation slightly amended, RB.
2. George Seferis, published in *Mythistorema,* 1935, poem 23: translation by RB. Mikis Theodorakis's song based on this poem belongs to his cycle *Epiphania,* 1970.

A Little Further, pp. 9-11

Dedicated to Jay Ramsay

This set of propositions is a truncated version of a longer piece prompted by observations about "tearing boundaries'" by Nikola Čobić in *The Wolf,* N°. 9, London, Spring 2005, pp. 43-5. The title refers back to the second epigraph.

Paragraph 1: "The centre cannot hold," W. B. Yeats, 'The Second Coming', 1919. Octavio Paz, see epigraph above.

Paragraph 4: Similarly, James Robertson translates Eng. '*magnanimity*' into Scots as '*weel-hertitness*' See *For Angus*, ed. Richard Berengarten and Gideon Calder, Los Poetry Press, Cambridge, 2009, p. xxi.

Paragraph 12: Archbishop Desmond Tutu, Foreword to *Exploring Forgiveness*, eds. Robert D. Enright and Joanna North, University of Wisconsin Press, Madison, 1998, p. xiii.

The Dialectics of Oxygen, pp. 12-13

Dedicated to Hadaa Sendoo

On Poetry and Glory (1), pp.14-16

Dedicated to Maria Filippakopoulou

Paragraph 11: 'Nowness' in German is *Jetztkeit*. See Norman Finkelstein, *Not One of Them in Place: Modern Poetry and Jewish-American Identity*, SUNY, New York, 2001, p. 99: "We are drawn into what Benjamin calls *Jetztkeit*, which he defines as the messianic 'time of the now', aware of previously hidden currents among ordinary experience." I came across this reference two days after writing this passage. See also Walter Benjamin, *Illuminations*, tr. Harry Zohn, Schocken Books, 1969, p. 26.

Paragraph 11: Richard Berengarten, *Under Balkan Light*, 2011, p. 75. See also 'Only the Common Miracle', *For the Living*, 2011, pp. 160-161. Both published by Shearsman Books, Exeter.

On Poetry and Glory (2), pp. 17-19

Dedicated to Theo Breuer

Paragraph 9: Rainer Maria Rilke,' The First Elegy', *Duino Elegies*, tr. J. B. Leishman and Stephen Spender, The Hogarth Press, London, 1939, pp.24-25. The original is:

> Denn das Schöne ist nichts
> als des Schrecklichen Anfang, den wir noch grade ertragen,
> und wir bewundern es so, weil es gelassen verschmäht,
> uns zu zerstören.

On Poetry and Catching Glories, pp. 20-22

Dedicated to Sara Poisson

Paragraph 5: "that willing suspension of disbelief for the moment, which constitutes poetic faith." Samuel Taylor Coleridge, *Biographia Literaria*, Chapter XIV, 1817.

Paragraph 6: Quotations are from: C.T. Onions, *The Oxford Dictionary of English Etymology*, Clarendon Press at Oxford University Press, Oxford, 1966; Rev. Walter. W. Skeat, *An Etymological Dictionary of the English Language*, Clarendon Press, Oxford, 3rd edition, 1898; and *The Compact Edition of the Oxford English Dictionary*, Oxford University Press, 1971.

Paragraph 8: Gershom E. Scholem, *Major Trends in Jewish Mysticism*, Routledge and Kegan Paul, London, 1969.

On Poetry and Magnanimity, pp. 23-26

Dedicated to Anthony Rudolf

Paragraph 11: "Poetry makes nothing happen." W. H. Auden, 'In memory of W. B. Yeats', 1939.

Cambridge,
June, 2012

Richard Berengarten: Bibliography

Selected Writings, Shearsman edition

Vol. 1	*For the Living : Selected Longer Poems, 1965–2000*	
Vol. 2	*The Manager*	
Vol. 3	*The Blue Butterfly*	*(The Balkan Trilogy, Part 1)*
Vol. 4	*In a Time of Drought*	*(The Balkan Trilogy, Part 2)*
Vol. 5	*Under Balkan Light*	*(The Balkan Trilogy, Part 3)*

Poetry

The Easter Rising 1967
The Return of Lazarus
Double Flute
Avebury
Inhabitable Space
Angels
Some Poems, Illuminated by Frances Richards
Learning to Talk
Tree
Roots/Routes
Black Light
Croft Woods
Against Perfection
Book With No Back Cover
Manual : the first 20
Holding the Darkness (*Manual: the second 20*)
Holding the Sea (*Manual: the third 20)*
Manual: the fourth 20

As Editor

An Octave for Octavio Paz
Ceri Richards : Drawings to Poems by Dylan Thomas
Rivers of Life
In Visible Ink : Selected Poems, Roberto Sanesi 1955-1979
Homage to Mandelstam
Out of Yugoslavia
For Angus
The Perfect Order: Selected Poems, Nasos Vayenas, 1974-2010

www.ingramcontent.com/pod-product-compliance
Lightning Source LLC
Chambersburg PA
CBHW032135050726
47590CB00008B/3110

* 9 7 8 1 8 4 8 6 1 3 1 2 6 *